Lose the Blanket, Linus!

LITTLE SIMON
An imprint of Simon & Schuster Children's Publishing Division
1230 Avenue of the Americas, New York, New York 10020
Copyright © 2003 United Feature Syndicate, Inc. All rights reserved.
PEANUTS is a registered trademark of United Feature Syndicate, Inc.
READY-TO-READ, LITTLE SIMON, and colophon are registered trademarks of Simon & Schuster.
Manufactured in the United States of America
2   4   6   8   10   9   7   5   3

Library of Congress Cataloging-in-Publication Data
Bailer, Darice.
Lose the blanket, Linus! / adapted by Darice Bailer.—1st ed.
p. cm. — (Peanuts ready-to-read)
"Based on the comic strips by Charles M. Schulz."
Summary: Lucy thinks Linus is too attached to his blanket
and wants to see what will happen to him without it.
ISBN 0-689-85472-2 (Paperback)
ISBN 0-689-85474-9 (Library Edition)
[1. Blankets—Fiction. 2. Brothers and sisters—Fiction.]
I. Schulz, Charles M. II. Title. III. Series.
PZ7.B1447 Lo 2003
[E]—dc21   2002003297

Lose the Blanket, Linus!

Based on the comic strips
by Charles M. Schulz
Adapted by Darice Bailer
Art adapted by Peter and Nick LoBianco

Ready-to-Read

Little Simon
New York   London   Toronto   Sydney   Singapore

Linus loved his blanket.
His sister, Lucy, didn't.
"You and that stupid blanket!"
Lucy said.
"It's not stupid," said Linus.

"Maybe if *you* had a blanket,
you wouldn't be so crabby,"
Linus said.
Lucy hit him.

Linus even took his blanket
to baseball practice.
He walked up to bat and swung.
CRACK!
"Run it out, Linus!"
yelled Charlie Brown.
"I have to have my blanket,"
Linus said.

Finally Linus ran to first base.
Then he ran toward second.
Lucy stomped on his blanket
and knocked him over.
Then she caught the ball
and tagged him.
"You are out!" she said.

Lucy really wanted Linus to
give up that blanket.
She called their blanket-hating
grandma. "Hello, Grandma,"
said Lucy. "Could you come
over to see us?"
Grandma said yes.

"Our blanket-hating grandma is
   coming," Lucy said. "She will
   be here this afternoon."
"Oh, no!" Linus said. "I am doomed!"

Grandma asked Linus what
was behind his back.
"Nothing," Linus said. "I mean,
nothing much."
Grandma told Linus to
hand over the blanket.
He didn't want to, but he did.

Lucy took the blanket
and made a kite.
"How could you do such a thing?"
asked Linus.
"Easy," Lucy said. Then she let go.
"You let go of it!" Linus yelled.
Lucy smiled. "Your blanket will be
the first to circle the moon!"

What if Linus's blanket landed
in the ocean?
"Oh, my poor blanket!"
Linus said.
"It can't swim!"
When Linus got his blanket back,
it was mad at Lucy.
It hissed at her and inched up
behind her.

14

"Auugh!" Lucy cried.
"It's attacking me! That stupid
blanket hates me! I am the only
kid I know who has ever been
attacked by a blanket!"

"I have had enough of that
blanket," said Lucy.
"Are you going to carry it around
for the rest of your life?
When are you going to learn
to stand on your own two feet?"

"What do you mean?" asked Linus.
"I do not need my blanket!
 I can give it up anytime I want to!
 Anytime!"

"I need your help,"
Linus told Snoopy.
"I want you to keep my blanket
for me and not give it back."
This is going to be fun,
thought Snoopy.

"Notice anything?" Linus asked Lucy.
"My blanket is gone! I gave it up!
  I do not need it anymore!"
  Then Linus started to shake.
"Good grief!" he said. "I want my
  blanket back!"

Snoopy liked taking care
of the blanket.
He sucked on his thumb
during the day.
He covered himself up at night.
He slept happily in the
moonlight.

But Linus could not sleep.
He missed his blanket.
"Is it morning yet?"
he asked Charlie Brown.
"No, it is only ten o'clock,"
said Charlie Brown.
"Only ten o'clock?"
Linus asked. "Good grief!"

"I want my blanket back!" Linus
told Snoopy. "I thought I could
give it up but I can't. . . .
I have to get it back!"
Snoopy stuck out his paw.
"I will take the blanket. . . .
You keep the thumb!" said Linus.

Lucy had tried everything.
Finally she hid her brother's blanket.
First she locked it in a closet.
Then she buried it.

Linus got out a shovel.
"I have to find my blanket,"
he told Charlie Brown.
Linus dug up one shovelful
of dirt. Then some more.
"I have to dig and dig until I
find it!" he said.

"Maybe I could get you
   something else," said Charlie Brown.
"Maybe I could get you a dish towel."
   Linus didn't want a dish towel.
   He wanted his blanket!
   He kept digging.

Lucy thought her little brother
would never find his blanket.
"I am going to find that blanket,
even if I have to dig up the whole
neighborhood!" Linus yelled.

"I will find it!" Linus yelled again.
But Lucy just walked away.
Snoopy helped look too,
and Snoopy found it.
"My blanket!" Linus shouted.
"Oh, Snoopy! You found it!"

Lucy was mad that
Snoopy found her brother's
blanket.
"Stupid dog!" she said.
Snoopy laughed.
"Hee-hee-hee!"

Linus was so happy that
he had his blanket back at last.
"My blanket! My good ol' blanket!"
he said. "It's been buried beneath the
ground. It's dirty. It's torn.
It's even a little moldy. . . ."

"But it's *my* blanket," said Linus.
Linus closed his eyes and sighed.

"Someday you are going to have to
  give up that blanket," Lucy said.
"Someday," Linus said.
"But not today."

August 2004